DEVOTIONS
for EVERYDAY
LIVING

RON HEMBREE

christian art gifts.

Preface

The telephone jangled nervously the other night nudging me from a gentle sleep. A faint voice at the other end of the line gasped, "I've just swallowed some pills. I think I'm going to die." Fortunately, the dose was not lethal.

Later another urgent call came from a mother whose son had been picked up by the police and she wanted me to do something about it. A young mother sat sobbing in my office saying she was plagued by all sorts of fears and needed help. She was afraid to die and afraid to live; afraid of sickness; afraid of people and afraid of God.

Two intelligent young people who once were deeply in love now glared at one another as they spat out accusations. They told me their marriage was through and all love they had once known was gone. The court could decide the fate of their two preschool children. I stood by the hospital bed of a dying alcoholic in the middle of the night. She was gasping for breath and her eyes jumped wildly around the room seeking an escape from the ominous visitor who had come for her. The torment and agony in those eyes would haunt me for many nights.

Cases such as these are not strange to ministers, doctors, and psychologists. However, all such cases point vividly to the fact that few know peace. We are living in the age of ulcers and aspirin. This is an age torn with tension and stabbed with strife. It is the age of the pill and the highball; the hollow laugh and the empty heart.

Lest we despair, there is an answer for such an age. Christ offers this in His sermons, His life, and His love. He actually promises us a personal tranquility in this age of ulcers and aspirin. By beginning each new day with His word, a thought, and a prayer, we can know this peace He promises. For this reason, I offer "Good Morning, Lord."

The thoughts and ideas are drawn from personal experience and from wisdom of those much wiser than I. However, basically the material is drawn from the simple, yet sublime teachings of our wonderful Savior. I trust these thoughts will be not just a diagnosis of problems but a prescription for peace and will turn some to the Prince of Peace.

~ Ron Hembree ~

Great love

"Love your enemies, bless them that curse you, do good to them that hate you, and pray for them which despitefully use you, and persecute you."
MATTHEW 5:44

In his book, *Christ in the Communist Prisons*, Richard Wurmbrand tells of the time his wife met the man who had murdered her family in Nazi Germany. She put her arms around him and as she wept she told him she had forgiven him. Such true and divinely given love can come only from a heart that knows it has been forgiven.

It is easy to show love to those we like or those of our own families. The real test of our relationship with Christ comes, however, when we move beyond our natural feelings to loving those whose actions have shown them to be our enemies. Some talk of "easy Christianity." There is no such thing. To be wholly like Christ is to be wholly unlike ourselves.

Circumstances, personality conflicts, tensions, or jealousies often bring us in conflict with our fellowmen. Some may show they do not like us, some may even determine to destroy us or our influence. In such situations we must call upon that divine love that lives in us to help us in our reactions. Then we will love not only the lovely, but also that one who is filled with hate.

Truth: Booker T. Washington once said, "I will permit no man to reduce my soul to the level of hatred."

Honest anyway

*The integrity of the upright shall
guide them: but the perverseness of
the transgressors shall destroy them.*
PROVERBS 11:3

Years ago in a southern slave market an intelligent looking Negro was put up for sale. A prospective buyer asked the young man, "If I buy you, will you be honest?" With a baffled expression the youth replied, "I will be honest whether or not you buy me."

There is that old expression, "Honesty pays." But it doesn't always pay in a tangible sense. Just because we return the money a clerk has mistakenly given us does not mean we will be given a monetary reward for our honesty.

There is, however, an intrinsic reward in our being honest, regardless of tangible results. God's Word speaks much of honesty from a pure heart, not seeking advantage but merely doing what is right because it *is* right.

We live in an age of cheaters and stealers. Tragically, the word *honesty* is almost forgotten in our culture. God remembers this word; and if we are to be His children we must remember, "The Lord rewarded me according to my righteousness; according to the cleanness of my hands hath He recompensed me" (Ps. 18:20).

*P*rayer: God, help me to remember that You desire truth in the inward parts of my soul.

Salt in the spring

"Ye are the salt of the earth: but if the salt have lost his savour, wherewith shall it be salted?"
MATTHEW 5:13

Elisha, fresh from a personal encounter with God, is met by men from a threatened city. Their water was stagnant and caused the ground to miscarry. Famine would soon wipe them out unless something was done. Knowing that Elisha was a prophet of God, they asked him to help them. Elisha simply said, "Bring me a cruse of salt," went to the head of the stream, and threw the salt in. From that day until this the stream in Jericho flows clean. God healed through the salt.

Christ often spoke in metaphors. One of

the strongest of these was "Ye are the salt of the earth." As Christ-centered people we influence those around us. As the people of Jericho found the water "naught," so our world has been disillusioned by the results of its own progress in science, philosophy, and materialism. We are threatened by a polluted "stream of meaninglessness." But Christ cast into this stream the "salt of the earth." Our "salting" influence has the potential to make the world rejoice again.

If ever the world desperately needed the influence of righteousness, it is now. Do not permit your "savour" to be taken from you by becoming mixed with the present world spirit. Remain pure – an influence for *good*.

*T*ruth: The world cannot survive a salt-free diet.

Perfect peace

Today's Scripture: Isaiah 26

*Thou wilt keep him in perfect
peace, whose mind is stayed on
Thee: because he trusteth in Thee.*
ISAIAH 26:3

A famous physician and professor at Harvard
Medical School asserts that 75 percent of the
healing work of the physician could be done
by the pastor. He was speaking of people who
have nothing organically wrong but who do
have very real physical symptoms. Permanent
cure of the psychosomatic lies in the treatment
of the whole man – body, mind, and spirit.

Per capita, the United States has more cases
of extreme mental illness than any other na-

tion in the world. One out of every twenty Americans can expect to be a patient in a mental institution sometime during his lifetime. One out of every five families will have to contend with the problem of alcohol.

For such an age as this there is a cure. It requires a proper inner life. God promises that if the seat of our lives, our thoughts, are centered on Him we will have perfect peace. Tragically, men are ignoring this age-old admonition and as a result they find their lives wrecked in self-explosion through excess. Happily, many have turned to Christ and there have found perfect peace. Yet even Christians at times let their minds wander, and when we peg our thoughts to something other than God, frustration results.

Prayer: Father, bring all my thoughts and imaginations into captivity to the obedience of Christ.

God's lawsuit

For the LORD hath a controversy
with the inhabitants of the land ...
HOSEA 4:1

A San Francisco man filed a lawsuit against God for damages during a recent earthquake. He holds God responsible and has actually hired an attorney to bring God to court concerning the matter. The case will probably have to be dropped because they can't find anyone to serve the subpoena.

This may be the first lawsuit filed against God, but it is not the first court action in which God has taken a part. One translation of this passage (*The Living Bible*) interprets our text for today thus, "God has filed

14

a lawsuit against Israel." The reasons are listed: "because there is no truth, no mercy, nor knowledge of God in the land." What a tragic situation! Violence naturally resulted, because men had lost their sense of direction and purpose. Life had become meaningless and the predominant philosophy was "Survival of the fittest."

We also live in a land where there is no truth, mercy, or knowledge of God. Our streets are filled with violence and each day it seems as though the wickedness of men reaches new depths. Men, having rejected God's Word as their foundation, know nothing but "meaninglessness." Pray for spiritual revival; pray, "Thy kingdom come."

Truth: In our age of guided missiles and misguided men we need the power and stability of God's eternal word.

Drugs as sacraments

———— ✐ ————

Today's Scripture: Matthew 24

*"When ye therefore shall see the
abomination of desolation, spoken
by Daniel the prophet, stand in
the holy place, (whoso readeth,
let him understand)."*
MATTHEW 24:15

Drug advocate Timothy Leary started a new
religion in which the taking of LSD is a sacrament, just as Christians partake of the bread
and cup of communion. From this a whole religious subculture has grown, in which drugs
are tools of worship and participants engage
in the basest sorts of sins and atrocities, even
to the point of murder. Naturally, serious
Christians are concerned about this desecra-

tion and feel it an abomination.

While we rightfully deplore these abominations, we should not be surprised, because Jesus said such things would come in the last days. He spoke of the "abomination of desolation." Holy men saw this first when Antiochus Epiphanes came to the throne in 175 B.C. He looted the Temple, set up a statue of Jupiter and sacrificed swine on the altars, insults which were followed by a frightful massacre. Jesus indicated there would be future abominations equal to this and would be one signal of the second coming of Christ.

Recently we have been seeing what seems to be the "ultimate abomination." It is at such a time as this that we need to reinforce our relationship with Christ. It is a time to pray, "Thy kingdom come."

*T*ruth: "When ye shall see all these things, know that it is near, even at the doors" (Matt. 24:33).

The undivorced

Today's Scripture: 1 Peter 3:1-9

*Finally, be ye all of one mind,
having compassion one of another.*
1 PETER 3:8

During a battle in Vietnam, two young men were in the thick of the fight. Bullets were flying overhead, shrapnel was bursting around them, and occasionally a grenade exploded nearby. One of the young men, terrified by the situation, gasped, "Isn't this awful?"

The other replied. "Oh, not really; it just reminds me of home."

Tragically, many homes in our land are torn with tension and strife. Some families are held together by convenience rather than love. Many people are not so much married as they are "undivorced." Because of this lack of love, violence spills over on our streets and takes a stranglehold on our society. We need a revival of love in the homes of our land.

Peter, married himself, gives some very practical advice to married folks. He speaks to each partner about individual responsibility and then sums it up by commanding that each have compassion for the other. He also warns that improper relationships can have deep spiritual implications, " … that your prayers be not hindered" (3:7).

Truth: Love in the home is a commandment of Christ.

Faithful friend

Today's Scripture: 2 Samuel 15:13-23

Surely in what place my lord the
king shall be, whether in death or life,
even there also will thy servant be.
2 SAMUEL 15:21

An aspiring young writer went to an old master for advice and wisdom. After giving the technical help sought the old writer said, "Son, remember your life is well spent if you can find only five real friends." The youth laughed and thought the old man senile. After all, he had many friends. However, years later, after many successes and failures the writer realized that the old master had been correct – except that five real friends were too many to expect. He had found only one.

We have many acquaintances but few friends. David had lost his best friend, Jonathan, years before, but here we glimpse another real friend God gave him. Ittai risked all, even death, to be with David. His words, recorded in this chapter, are too sincere to suspect political advantage on Ittai's part. At this time defeat was sure, yet he said, "In death or life, I want to be with you."

This is a lonely world and when we, who know the friend that sticketh closer than a brother, befriend mankind, we indeed fulfill one of the greatest missions of man. Let us be friends and brothers to lonely people.

Truth: "A friend loveth at all times, and a brother is born for adversity" (Prov. 17:17).

Bread on water

Today's Scripture: Ecclesiastes 11:1-6

Cast thy bread upon the waters: for thou shalt find it after many days.
ECCLESIASTES 11:1

At planting time the great Nile River over-flows, flooding the cropland. Farmers take the tiny seed and wade through the waters, sowing in flooded fields. At the time it seems as though their efforts will be wasted. How-ever, when the waters recede and the sun warms the soil these tiny seeds, which sank in the water, spring forth.

In the midst of a book, which cries out, "Vanity of vanities, all is vanity," there is hidden one of the most important truths of God's Word. There are times in our life when

who are of his particular church or denomination. With full maturity comes an interest in and love for all of the household of faith.

Peter's last command to early Christians was that they should grow up. Too often we are interested only in ourselves or our little circle of friends. God would have us learn that there are many others who have not "bowed their knees to Baal." Christian maturity will bring a oneness in heart and spirit between people of all faiths and races. As we learn to know God better we begin to realize just how deeply He loves all men.

*P*rayer: Help my love and concern to be world encompassing and help me realize there are men of great faith in all churches.

Prince of Peace

Glory to God in the highest, and on earth peace, good will toward men.
LUKE 2:14

Dawn came, that morning during World War I, but fog lay so heavy on the battlefield that visibility was almost zero. When the fog finally lifted it became apparent that the French had advanced somewhat while the Germans had retreated a bit. Between the lines of battle lay a lonely farmhouse. Bullets whizzed over it.

Suddenly both sides stopped firing. A toddler had emerged from the house and was playing unafraid in the yard. Not a soldier on either side would fire a shot until that baby had been taken to safety. For a moment the baby had brought peace.

Christ came to bring ultimate peace to mankind. Sometimes we despair and wonder how long anger and evil will be allowed to reign. However, God promised that the tiny baby of Bethlehem, the Prince of Peace, will establish a Kingdom of peace. On a personal level all Christians already know the inner peace this Christ gives. We have the promise that one day all men will bow down to Him, the Lord of lords and King of kings. Until that beautiful day arrives we are challenged and commanded to let the peace of God reign in our hearts.

*T*ruth: "The wrong shall fail, the right prevail with peace on earth, good will toward men."

For love

⟋⟍⟍

Today's Scripture: 2 Corinthians 5

For the love of Christ constraineth us …
2 CORINTHIANS 5:14

Years ago a young country doctor was making his regular sick calls when a violent thunderstorm arose. The farmer on whom the doctor was calling begged the young man to stay through the night. "If you leave now," the farmer said, "You'll never make it home. The paths will be flooded. Your horse might lose his footing and you would fall down the steep slopes." "I cannot stay," said the physician, "My wife is waiting for me. I know she will be frightened in this storm and I must get home to her." He risked his life because he loved his wife more than he loved himself.

Love such as this has always inspired man. Paul the apostle had a similar love for God. He had gone through the fire and the flood for his Christ, whom he loved deeply. In this majestic chapter he clearly defines his motives for endangering his life so many times, "The love of Christ constraineth us."

Many of us have not yet felt the intense drive of such love for Christ. Don't be too hard on yourself. At the start of their association with Christ, the apostles also questioned whether they would be able to stand. They grew deeply in Christ to the point where nothing could stop their message, not even the threat of death. The truth is that we too can and must grow just as deeply in our love for the Savior.

Prayer: Deepen my love until I am "constrained" to give all for the Master.

Life is

Today's Scripture: 2 Timothy 1:6-13

But is now made manifest by the appearing of our Saviour Jesus Christ, who hath abolished death, and hath brought life and immortality to light through the gospel.
2 Timothy 1:10

The controversial clergyman, the late Dr. Harry Emerson Fosdick, talked often of death and immortality, "For me," he said, "immortality belongs to the only family of ideas that makes sense of the universe. Without it you have a purposeless world whose ultimate symbol is a closed door. With every fiber of my being I believe in the purposefulness of life. Like sunshine, which we don't think about but which is here, a conviction runs through me that spiritual life is eternal and that ahead of it, doors are open. That is all we need to know."

For centuries men have pondered life beyond the grave. Then Jesus came and by His example of death and resurrection proved beyond any doubt the veracity of the afterlife. And, as Dr. Fosdick noted, "all of life now makes sense."

One day Jesus confronted the Sadducees, who denied immortality, with the fact that whenever the term "God of Abraham, Isaac, and Jacob" is used in Scripture, it is always in the present tense. These individuals, then, are alive and aware right now in another world. The Mount of Transfiguration experience again proved eternal life. Death is a doorway, not a termination point.

*T*ruth: Because He lives we also will live.

God's peace pill

Today's Scripture: Philippians 4:19

*And the peace of God, which passeth
all understanding, shall keep your
hearts and minds through Jesus Christ.*
PHILIPPIANS 4:7

Psychologists estimate that each week thirty-three thousand Americans who have no organic illness see a doctor. Their emotional conflicts have resulted in physical symptoms. They are evidence that this is an age of troubled hearts, empty souls and lost lives. For these ills many doctors prescribe tranquilizers, for they do not realize that true personal peace can come only through faith in Christ.

Paul, writing to the Philippians, wraps up his epistle with excellent words of advice concerning a proper relationship with Christ and a proper inner life. He talks about right thinking and confidence in the Christ who gives peace beyond human comprehension.

Paul assures us we need "Be careful for nothing; but in every thing by prayer and supplication with thanksgiving let your requests be made known unto God" (v. 6). If we have a deep faith in our Christ and the inner knowledge that everything that happens to us is controlled by a loving Father, then the frustrations and vicissitudes of life will not tear our spirits; instead they will help us grow in peace and confidence toward Him.

*P*rayer: Lord, let me have a peace to stand and a power to change.

Stolen money

Repent ye therefore, and be converted,
that your sins may be blotted out.
Acts 3:19

Jim asked his friend Tom to drop off a deposit at the bank for him. Instead Tom spent the money, and began to evade Jim. Years passed. Their relationship, of course, became strained. One day Tom decided he missed the companionship of his old friend. He didn't admit stealing Jim's money but merely tried to reestablish the relationship with Jim. It didn't work, for Jim could not rightly trust Tom.

Following Peter's fiery sermon, convicted sinners asked, "What must we do?" Peter immediately advised that there must be public acknowledgement of sin and disobedience if ever a friendly relationship is to develop between God and man.

There are people today who would like to merely "turn over a new leaf" and ignore past sins. But this doesn't work. Man must repent, acknowledge his wrong, and right his action before a meaningful relationship develops. Repentance and restitution are keys to happy living.

Truth: The psychiatrist's couch can never replace the mourner's bench.

No light in the lamp

Today's Scripture: 2 Timothy 4:1-8

Preach the word:
be instant in season, out of season.
2 TIMOTHY 4:2

In the years before automatic train signals were installed at railroad crossings there were many tragic accidents. One involved a family out for a pleasure drive late at night. They were all killed.

The railroad company appointed a board of inquiry, which called on the watchman who was assigned to that crossing. "Didn't you wave your lantern?" They asked. "Yes!" responded the man.

However, later he admitted that although he had waved the lantern there had been no light in it. The oil had run out and he hadn't taken the time to refill it.

Paul wrote to Timothy, the young preacher, and urged him to never lose his sense of urgency. He admonished him to wave the light of warning at all times. But he also indicated that there must be something more than urgency; there must be the full anointing of God. In verse 5 he says, "Make full proof of thy ministry." This means to not only preach, but to preach with anointing.

In our day of ulcers and aspirin remember to never lose your sense of urgency. However, we must keep in mind that a lantern without light is useless, Paul said. "Take heed unto thyself." Be filled with His Spirit.

Truth: "Watchman, what of the night?" (Isa. 21:11)

Time is an enemy

―――――― ∞ ――――――

Today's Scripture: Ecclesiastes 3:1-8

To every thing there is a season, and a
time to every purpose under the heaven.
ECCLESIASTES 3:1

"Hours and Flowers Soon Fade Away," are the doleful words inscribed on the giant floral clock in the heart of St. Louis, Missouri's Forest Park. Though mournful, these words do express the sad fact that time is a bitter enemy of creatures on this globe. Just yesterday we were enjoying the freedoms of childhood; today we are enjoying the fruit of our work; and tomorrow we will be bent and gray. Because time is an enemy we need to establish priorities in our lives.

The Preacher in Ecclesiastes seems to suggest that there is an eternal time schedule. "There is a time to laugh … a time to sow." God wills that we have a well-adjusted and joyful life. However, Satan would disturb this divine timetable by having us waste precious moments and over-emphasize our times of pleasure. It is easy to yield to the temptations of making life a *game* rather than a *workshop*.

Daily commitment to Christ and a well-disciplined life in the Spirit can keep time from being our enemy. Make time your friend by doing daily what Christ desires.

*P*rayer: Lord, let me do what You wish me to do today.

Making of men

⟨ ⟩

Today's Scripture: Hebrews 12:1-11

Looking unto Jesus the author
and finisher of our faith.
HEBREWS 12:2

Michelangelo felt called of God to wrest figures from stone. As master sculptor, he gave us such great works as *David, the Pieta,* and *Moses.*

His drive to free forms from stony prisons is but a shadow of the Great Artist, God, in developing man's spiritual life. God wants us "to be conformed to the image of His Son" (Rom. 8:29). And discipline is a part of that process. "Being punished isn't enjoyable while it is happening ... it hurts! But afterwards we can see the result, a quiet growth in grace and character" (v. 11, *The Living Bible*). As the sculptor chips away ugly stone, God cuts away that which is unlike Christ in our lives.

We are flesh, and cutting hurts. Therefore we also need the loving touch of our Great Physician. Through discipline we grow in grace to become like His Son.

Job, undergoing great sorrow, said, "Thine hands have made me and fashioned me together round about; yet Thou dost destroy me. Remember I beseech Thee, that Thou has made me as the clay" (Job 10:8, 9).

*P*rayer: Lord, help me to feel not only the chisel's bite, but also the Physician's touch. Forgive me for resenting discipline. I know that You know what is best for me each day.

Dear Abby

Today's Scripture: 1 Samuel 25

And David said to Abigail,
Blessed be the Lord God of Israel,
which sent thee this day to meet me.
1 Samuel 25:32

The bullet Aaron Burr pumped into the body of Alexander Hamilton not only killed his long-time foe, but also signaled the end of Burr's political and social life. The American people would not tolerate a man in such high position acting so totally out of character with the dignity of his office and the principles of righteousness. Aaron Burr's name has since been associated with that which is cowardly, despicable, and evil.

David might have acted in the same manner

had it not been for a beautiful woman named Abigail. Tension mounted in those days following Samuel's death. Saul was determined to kill David, and David's raw-edged nerves drove him to anger and frustration. When Nabal refused a common courtesy, David hastily decided to kill him. Abigail, the peacemaker, came and pleaded with David not to act out of character with his godly conviction. David listened and tragedy was averted.

There may be times when tension drives us to act out of character with our convictions. Thank God there is usually an Abigail who soothes us and helps us remember our high calling. It is important that each of us act as our brother's keeper, taking the role of Abigail, helping him in his time of stress.

Truth: "Blessed are the peacemakers: for they shall be called the children of God" (Matt. 5:9).

Defeat

Today's Scripture: 1 Samuel 28:7-25

*Because thou obeyedst not the voice
of the LORD, ... therefore hath the LORD
done this thing unto thee this day.*
1 SAMUEL 28:18

In the last decaying days of the Third Reich, Hitler acted out of panic and gave orders no responsible man would ever have given. Albert Speer, in his memoirs, tells of those falling days and how Hitler degenerated from a powerful leader of uncanny strength to a shaky old man burned out before his years. Trying to save the shreds of his dreams, Hitler destroyed many lives.

Saul, the bright young man with a promising future, decided he alone was able to lead

Israel. He ignored God only to find that without His strength, fondest dreams are cruelly crushed. Still, egocentric, he vacillated, flirting with repentance, then rejected godliness in favor of his own pursuit. Now the kingdom was falling and in desperation he resorted to witchcraft. This dark act spelled final doom for the pathetic Saul. Death lay but days away.

Sin has a decaying effect. There is a progression of evil – "Then when lust hath conceived, it bringeth forth sin: and sin, when it is finished, bringeth forth death" (James 1:15). Let's realize that the only *positive* progression comes when we grow "in the vine." In Him we move and have our being. When we separate ourselves from Him, decay and death result.

*T*ruth: "As the branch cannot bear fruit of itself, except it abide in the vine; no more can ye, except ye abide in Me" (John 15:4).

Tell the good

Today's Scripture: 2 Samuel 1

*Tell it not in Gath, publish it not
in the streets of Askelon; lest the
daughters of the Philistines rejoice ...*
2 SAMUEL 1:20

Recently an imaginative reporter got fed up with all the bad news being reported across the nation. He compiled an amazing list of statistics carried by major news agencies about all the people who would *not* be arrested, would *not* rob, would *not* murder, would *not* riot, and would *not* burn down universities and banks. His article had an impact; it showed that many times we do concentrate only on that which is negative.

When Saul died the people immediately

began to rejoice that his rule of terror was ended. They no doubt felt this would flatter David, the heir apparent. To their amazement he was not pleased and lamented the death of the king and his son. In his song of lamentation the goodnesses of Saul and Jonathan was exalted and their weaknesses ignored. David did not want the world to see the weaknesses of God's people.

Often when we Christians spot weaknesses in one another, we are quick to expose these. However, David's admonition is still valid. The world rejoices to see the faults of the church and Christians. Let us not give Satan reason to laugh; let us talk of the great and good in others and ignore their faults.

$\mathcal{T}$ruth: "Speak evil of no man" (Titus 3:2).

Stolen lamb

Today's Scripture: 2 Samuel 12

And Nathan said to David, Thou art the man.
2 SAMUEL 12:7

Two boys were fighting bitterly over a broken toy. Finally one shouted, "It's time one of us acted like a Christian. Why don't you?" Strange how we can insist that the other person be righteous but ignore the evil within ourselves.

An old prophet reported an injustice to King David. It seems a wealthy shepherd stole the single lamb of a poor citizen. David, angered by such injustice demanded, "As the Lord liveth, the man that hath done this thing shall surely die." Pointing a finger in the face of the boiling king, Nathan said, "Thou art the man!" David is staggered as he is suddenly convicted of his sin with Bathsheba. In bitter tears he asked forgiveness for the terrible sins he had compounded by his own unchecked lust. God forgave, but David "reaped what he sowed" as he saw the results of his sin worked out in his own family.

Jesus warned of a self-righteousness so blinding that we cannot see the "beam in our own eye." It is well to remember that we are called to be helpers of mankind, not judges. We are all so far from perfect that not one of us is qualified to sit in judgment on someone else's righteousness. It is so easy to demand righteousness in others, but excuse our sins as weaknesses.

*T*ruth: "Judge not, that ye be not judged" (Matt. 7:1).

Exorcism

Today's Scripture: Mark 16:14-20

In my name shall they cast out devils.
MARK 16:17

Redlands University professor, Dr. William R. Parker said that when he returned from World War II his life was outwardly ideal but inwardly in turmoil. The campus was serene, his daughters, a joy, and there was no obvious discord or strain. However, although he was a psychologist, he was plagued with what he called "four demons," *hate, fear, inferiority,* and *guilt.* This drove him to a scientific research on the power of prayer and his life was changed. The demons were exorcised.

In the colorful language of the New Testament, many inner turmoils and conflicts were

50

termed "demon possession." Christ, Master of all of earth and nature, said we need not be slaves to these churning emotions and promised He would give us power to cast them out of our lives. These last words of Christ are particularly meaningful in our century of confusion and uncertainty.

As Dr. Parker discovered, there is power in prayer. As we submit ourselves completely to Him in periods of inner inspection and then look to Him for effective change, our lives become different. We no longer are tormented by these frustrating "demons" but live in clean houses in the company of the King of kings.

*T*ruth: There is no power that can conquer you while you are on Christ's side.

Power of influence

Today's Scripture: Acts 6

And all that sat in the council,
looking steadfastly on him, saw his
face as it had been the face of an angel.
ACTS 6:15

Sixty years ago a sociology class predicted the fate of two hundred slum children. After careful interviews they concluded that 96 percent of these children would spend time in jail. Fifty-three years later a follow-up was made. It revealed that only four had ever done time. Why had so many succeeded in overcoming their bad environment? Almost all of them said, "There was a teacher who loved me and inspired me to goodness."

Echoes of influence from Stephen's short

life reverberated long after angry cries of "Kill him!" died down. Young Paul was no doubt touched by that influence, as were all those who saw his face as "that of an angel." The impact of that one life shattered the false religion of that day and subsequently influenced history.

Often we think our contribution to life is minimal. But like the life of the slum teacher, and of the first martyr, our lives have a deep impact on others. While we may not be privileged to see the tremendous circle of influence we have, yet we can be sure that our lives are deeply influential. Live responsibly, and be an influence for Christ.

*T*ruth: The shadow of one Christ-centered life falls far into the future of mankind.

Religion explosion

⎯⎯⎯ ◦ ⎯⎯⎯

Today's Scripture: Acts 5

Did not we straitly command you that ye should not teach in this name? and, behold, ye have filled Jerusalem with your doctrine.

Acts 5:28

Mussolini, for political purposes, severely persecuted the church in prewar Italy. Pastors were arrested and exiled to farming communities away from population centers. The Italian dictator hoped by this action to wipe out the church. However, wherever these pastors went they continued to witness and as a direct result today there are churches all over Italy.

Opponents of Christianity have always underestimated the power of the Gospel. In the apostles' day they expected that a stern rebuke, a beating, perhaps a death, would wipe out the church. They found instead that persecution added fuel to the fire and the number of those who believed the Gospel grew.

At times we fear persecution as a threat to our church. However, the pattern has always been that in times of tension, the church moves forward with great strides. The stories filtering out from behind the Iron Curtain prove that the church there is still a force to be reckoned with. Persecution purifies, preserves, and challenges true believers in the Lord. This fulfills the promise that hell's gates will not prevail against the church.

*T*ruth: Fire has not quenched and the sword has not stopped the surging tide of spiritual revival.

Power of prayer

Today's Scripture: Acts 4

And when they heard that, they lifted up their voices to God with one accord.
Acts 4:24

During the 1930 Communistic uprising in China, Dr. Walter H. Judd spent tense times there as a medical missionary. For eight months he was in polite captivity with clothes packed in case of emergency evacuation. He said the one thing that sustained him through these times was prayer. He explained, "There would come into my spirit something that supported and held me steady, gave me confidence and assurance during the day."

During those tense days of persecution of the early church, it is interesting to note what an important part prayer played in the lives of the apostles. Immediately after their first encounter with bitter opposition, they went to the Lord in prayer concerning the matter. They believed deeply in the sustaining power of an active prayer life.

Times have not changed a great deal. Although our opposition may not be overt, yet Satan still oppresses; and in times like these the dynamic power of a close relationship with Christ through prayer sustains us. Through uninterrupted communication with Christ we become stronger disciples. Prayer provides power for any occasion.

Truth: The fastest way to God is on one's knees.

Marbles and water

Cee

Today's Scripture: Acts 2

Then they that gladly received His word were baptized: and the same day there were added about three thousand souls.

ACTS 2:41

The object of the chemistry instructor was to teach by means of experiments the differences between "mixtures" and "compounds." He dropped marbles into a glass of water and stirred, then allowed it to settle. Result: Marbles and water. This, he said, is a "mixture." Then he added sugar to water in another glass and stirred. The sugar dissolved and no settling occurred. Two ingredients had combined to make a solution that did not separate. This, he explained, is a "compound."

Many treat religion as if it were a "mixture." They have heard of God, attend services, read about religion; but basically it is not a meaningful part of their lives. Those who experienced Pentecost, however, found their lives changed. They had encountered Christ and they became totally absorbed in God and His work. No longer was religion a casual part of their lives.

Just as at Pentecost, men today can have the dynamic experience of a personal encounter with the living Christ. Religion then becomes more than an activity separate from the vital issues of our existence. Christ becomes the living center of our very lives. We are one with Him.

*T*ruth: Christ is the living center of our faith and lives.

Lions, snakes, and dragons

Today's Scripture: Psalm 91

Thou shalt tread upon the lion and adder:
the young lion and the dragon
shalt thou trample under feet.
Psalm 91:13

Metaphors are time bombs, set to explode. When faith and truth mix there is an explosion of knowledge in one's spirit from the riches of God's Word. Here three metaphors are used: lions, snakes, and dragons. The lion represents trouble, seen and expected. God gives us victory over these. Snakes generally attack without warning. They speak of unexpected heartbreak. God also supplies grace in these troubles and brings us through to victory. Then there are the dragons – imaginary creatures. They represent those things in life that are not real, the things we imagine, the "possibilities" that frighten us.

We know that we will meet lions in our lives. Death is part of life; so is sickness. These are troubles we all expect, and God will give us strength to overcome. The snakes are more terrifying – the sudden loss of a child or a mate, perhaps; or maybe we lose our financial security through circumstances beyond our control. Again, Christ will help us through. We must deal with those undefined nagging fears, our "dragons," by relying on the positive power of Jesus Christ – "Be anxious in nothing … "

God's Word states that we shall "tread on lions, snakes, and dragons." This speaks of absolute and complete victory. There is a great finality in our victory through Him.

*T*ruth: "We are more than conquerors through Him that loved us" (Rom. 8:37).

Pardon rejected

Today's Scripture: Romans 10:9-13

For whosoever shall call upon the name of the Lord shall be saved.
ROMANS 10:13

President Andrew Jackson pardoned George Wilson after he was sentenced to hang for robbing the mail and for murder. However, Wilson refused the pardon, so the Supreme Court was called in to decide his fate. Chief Justice John Marshall gave the decision, "A pardon is a paper, the value of which depends upon its acceptance by the person implicated. George Wilson must be hanged." And he was.

How foolish for a man to reject a pardon, especially when his life is involved. Yet, every day there are thousands who are doing just this. In Romans Paul sets down clearly the great pardon from eternal death, which God has provided. It is so simple. All man has to do is, "Confess with thy mouth the Lord Jesus ... and believe in thine heart that God hath raised Him from the dead." Yet, foolishly, man consciously or unconsciously, rejects that pardon.

Those who have accepted the great pardon find it is more than just an escape from death. Other rich and meaningful blessings await them, those of peace and fellowship with God and the beginning of a new life filled with deep and abiding joy. The pardon Christ gives includes eternal fellowship along with forgiveness.

*T*ruth: So great a salvation, so rich and so free.

Sin costs

~~~~~~~~~~~~~~~~~~~

Today's Scripture: Isaiah 43:1-7

*Fear not: for I have redeemed thee, I have
called thee by thy name; thou art mine.*
ISAIAH 43:1

A Nevada youth was stopped by a police-
man in a routine investigation. Angered, he
grabbed a pistol and shot. The officer died.
Today the youth faces a life sentence behind
bars. His moment of anger cost him his freedom forever.

God tried to communicate the cost of
sin to Israel. "I gave Egypt and Ethiopia and
Seba in exchange for your freedom, as your
ransom. Others died that you might live ... "
(v. 3, 4, *The Living Bible*). Man has always ignored the cost of sin. Even bloody animal

sacrifices, repulsive to us, failed to convey effectively how God detests sin. Sins of fathers are visited on their children through inherited environment and weakened bodies. There is always a heavy price tag on sin.

In our age of spiritual apathy we see sin accepted as weakness rather than wickedness. Tragically, future generations will pay for our sins and many lives may be sacrificed because of us. How dreadful it will be to stand before God and give an account of our selfish sins!

*P*rayer: Lord, forgive my sins and forgive me for bringing grief on those about me because of my selfish ways. Help me to be "Christ-centered" rather than self-centered.

The mystery printer

Today's Scripture: Luke 12:22-31

"But rather seek ye the kingdom of God; and all these things shall be added unto you."
<small>LUKE 12:31</small>

A shabbily dressed transient recently dropped dead on a street in a Midwestern city. When his body was removed to the morgue it was discovered he had thirteen hundred dollars pinned to his underwear. Further investigation revealed he was a printer who had lived as a recluse without friends or family, hoarding all he could get. He was buried by the state and the government got his money.

This true but tragic story reminds us that men often place values on wrong things. The dead recluse had scrambled values. If he had sought to be a helper of humanity rather than withdrawing from life, his story would have had a far different conclusion.

Jesus often spoke about the dangers of materialism. He daily pointed to the tragedy of lives lost and souls damned because men have misplaced values. His clarion call was for man to seek first the kingdom of God. In our society of plenty we tend to get wrapped up with "things", forgetting the weightier matters of life. Oh, that we might deeply absorb Christ's message and meaning when He states, "The life is more than meat, and the body is more than raiment."

Prayer: Father, help us keep our values centered on eternal matters, only on those things which really matter.

If he were mine

────────── ✑ ──────────

Today's Scripture: Hosea 11:1-9

*And my people are bent to backsliding
from me: though they called them to the
most High, none at all would exalt him.*
HOSEA 11:7

Scarcely had he been released from prison
when the youth broke parole and was arrested
again. Speaking to the grieving father, a friend
said, "He's caused you so much trouble. If he
were my son I would forget him." To this the
loving parent responded, "Yes, if he were your
son I, too, would forget him. But, you see,
he's my son."

Hosea captures the very "human" hurt of
God whose love is rejected by those He cre-
ated. In pronouncing judgment God weeps,

"Oh, how can I give you up, My Ephraim? How can I let you go? … My heart cries out within Me; How I long to help you" (v. 8, *The Living Bible*). We have given God many reasons to give us up, yet He has pledged Himself to us because we are His.

Who can understand the depths of God's love covering our myriad faults and supplying our urgent needs? The songwriter said,

> Tho I forget Him and wander away,
> Still He doth love me wherever I stray;
> Back to His dear loving arms I would flee,
> When I remember that Jesus loves me.

It is comforting to know God loves us in spite of our terrible weaknesses.

*P*rayer: Lord, let me never use Your love as license for evil in my life. Rather, may I learn to live so my life will be worthy of Your companionship every day.

Computer marriage

———— ◦◦◦ ————

Today's Scripture: Genesis 24

... and he loved her: And Isaac was comforted after his mother's death.
GENESIS 24:67B

A young couple was recently married after having been introduced by an IBM computer. Their physical characteristics, personality traits, backgrounds and mental prowess were fed into the computer and were matched.

While matchmaking by machine is an innovation, yet matching rather than selection is not new. One of the first cases of matchmaking was by Abraham who chose his son's bride. Today's youth would object to such matchmaking. They want to make their own selection. However, before the story is ignored there is an important truth to learn.

Successful marriage is not just *finding* the right mate, but *becoming* the right mate. Abraham knew the marriage of his son would work because he had built character into his son that would make him the right kind of husband.

In our age of soaring divorce rates it is imperative that each partner strive to make his marriage work by becoming the right kind of marriage partner. God's Word speaks much of the marriage relationship and emphasizes the role each should play in developing a proper Christ-like spirit which will ensure the success of his marriage.

*P*rayer: Lord, make me a loving Christ-like marriage partner.

Christic in crisis

——— ⟿ ———

Today's Scripture: Hosea 2:14-23

*And I will give her ... the valley
of Achor for a door of hope.*
HOSEA 2:15

It was in the valley of Achor that Achan was stoned for his sin. Since that time the valley has been associated with trouble, heartbreak, and disappointment. Those traveling the spiritual valley of Achor are in the tension of crisis. Yet, God promises help even here.

Many today are walking through the valley of trouble. Each person has his special valley and the sorrow in some is deeper and darker than in others. The valley can be brightened only by the "Sun of Righteousness." He said, "Come unto Me, all ye that labour and are heavy laden, and I will give you rest. Take My yoke upon you, and learn of Me; for I am meek and lowly in heart: and ye shall find rest unto your souls" (Matt. 11:28-29).

To live by the law of Christ and accept Him in our hearts is to turn a giant floodlight of hope into our valleys of trouble. Problems do not always vanish in Christ's presence, but He gives us victory over them. "My grace is sufficient for thee: for My strength is made perfect in weakness" (2 Cor. 12:9).

Truth: Lord, I would clasp Thy hand in mine,
    Nor ever murmur nor repine,
    Content, whatever lot I see,
    Since 'tis my God that leadeth me.

Valley of death

———— ⌘ ————

Today's Scripture: Psalm 23

Yea, though I walk through the valley of the shadow of death, I will fear no evil: for thou art with me; thy rod and thy staff they comfort me.
PSALM 23:4

In Israel there actually is a valley known as the Valley of the Shadow of Death. It is very narrow and treacherous; its walls extend upward fifteen hundred feet, and the valley floor has many gullies. The paths in many places are so narrow the sheep cannot turn around. About halfway through the valley, the path is cut in two by an eight-foot gully. Wild dogs lurk in the valley and make it a most fearful place for the sheep.

The words of the psalm take on new meaning when we think of this valley. The road of life leading toward the valley of the shadow is dark and frightening. There is much to harm us and there are many deep pitfalls along the way. Then there is that break in the path, which signals the end of this life and the start of another. Those who walk without the Shepherd take a fearful leap in the dark and hope to make it.

Christ, the Good Shepherd is with His sheep in the valley and leads us through to eternal life. He never leaves nor forsakes.

*T*ruth: "I will fear no evil: for Thou art with me" (Ps. 23:4).

Reactions

— ℰℓℓℯ —

Today's Scripture: Luke 15:25-32

*Not rendering evil for evil, or railing
for railing: but contrariwise
blessing; knowing that ye are thereunto
called, that ye should inherit a blessing.*
1 PETER 3:9

Every day on the streets we meet the old Yankee's philosophy:

Ef you want peace, the thing you've got tu du
Is jes' to show you're up to fightin' tu.

Christ, however, told of turning the other cheek, going the second mile. Our reactions are not to be determined by another's actions; rather, our testimony should be demonstrated by our deeds.

In our relationship with others, all of us at times are tempted to harbor feelings and emotions that are spiritually destructive. Most often these attitudes originate in a deep-seated sense of insecurity or inadequacy, and manifest themselves in animosity.

It is easy to become jealous of someone who seems more blessed than we, especially if we feel more deserving. Such was the reaction of the elder brother in Luke 15. The result was a severing of a relationship. But these emotions have no place in the attitude of a Christian.

*T*ruth: We are called to be thermostats instead of thermometers, *affecting* our environment, not *reflecting* it.

Knowing and doing

———— ∞ ————

Today's Scripture: James 2

What doth it profit, my brethren,
though a man say he hath faith, and
have not works? Can faith save him?
JAMES 2:14

Thirty people stood watching as a diesel engine roared toward a deaf man walking between the railroad tracks. Some screamed. Others gasped. A man waved his newspaper, trying to warn the victim. A woman wept. Suddenly a young man leaped out of the crowd, ran across the tracks and threw his body against the man. The train thundered by, missing them by inches.

Thirty people saw the need, yet only one did anything about it. James seems to be saying here that if we really love God and have deep faith we will be moved to action to try to relieve the heartbreak of the world through Christ. It is not enough to *know*, we also must *do*.

Another apostle talked about being moved to action. John states, "My little children; let us not love in word, neither in tongue; but in deed and in truth" (1 John 3:18). Real love and faith not only sees or says but also moves on to relieve those needs through positive Christ-centered action.

*P*rayer: Lord, make me not just a hearer and believer of Your Word, but also a *doer*.

The dead heir

———— ·C~· ————

Today's Scripture: Acts 17:22-34

And the times of this ignorance
God winked at; but now commandeth
all men every where to repent.
Acts 17:30

A Californian who would not believe his only son was killed in World War II left half of his $25 million fortune to the dead son. The boy was reported missing in action; afterward his body was found and identified, but the father refused to accept the fact of his son's death.

How foolish to hold on to a hopeless dream! Some people are holding on to a dream even more foolish and more fantastic. Many live, think, and speak as though there is no punishment for sins and no vindication for wickedness. They hold to the hopeless dream that the Bible is wrong when it says, "The soul that sinneth, it shall die."

God demands that all repent. Ignorance is no excuse for evil and all men will one day stand before God to give an account for the deeds they have done in the flesh. That appointed day comes for each man and it is a wise individual who realizes he must make things right with his Maker.

*P*rayer: May our account of sin be settled by the blood of Calvary's Lamb.

The ice and the eagle

Today's Scripture: Romans 6

*For the wages of sin is death; but the gift of God
is eternal life through Jesus Christ our Lord.*
ROMANS 6:23

One day a giant eagle was flying over an
icy river. Spotting a floating carcass, the bird
swept down and sank his huge talons into the
cold flesh and began to eat. The river flowed
swiftly toward a plunging waterfall, but why
should the eagle worry, for at any moment he
could fly from the freezing carcass.

Just as the carcass went over the edge the
huge bird stretched his strong wings. But his
talons had frozen in the icy flesh of the dead
animal. Screaming, and flapping his wings,
the eagle plunged over the falls to his death.

Evil habits grip us in much the same way. We think we will be able to shed them any time we please – only to find that while we were preoccupied with our own strength, they have taken a death hold on us. The wise person recognizes the strength of sin and shuns involvement with that which is evil. For the one already trapped by foolish habits the power of Christ is available. He can make us new creatures in Him.

Prayer: Jesus, keep me near the cross.

The compelling Christ

Today's Scripture: Mark 1:16-20

And straightway they forsook
their nets, and followed him.
MARK 1:18

The late Dr. Peter Marshall often told of a New York fish vendor who had a shop in a main marketplace. One day a dark tall stranger walked into the shop and said, "Joe, I want you to follow me." Without a question the seller of fish closed up his shop, never to open it again, left his family, and followed the stranger.

Dr. Marshall would then say, "You think this strange. Was this not what Christ did to the disciples?" There must have been a tremendous attraction about the Christ for twelve men to forsake friend, family, and occupation just because He said, "Follow Me." Christ promised them nothing. He had no money to give them. He could promise them only hardships and trials. They followed because they knew they had at last found the Christ.

The same thing happens when you meet the compelling Christ. Things you thought important before suddenly lose their importance. The same power that caused the twelve to leave all compels you to give a selfless service to Him.

Truth: All things change when you find the Savior.

Keepers of Kin

Today's Scripture: Genesis 14:14-24

And he brought back all the goods, and also brought again his brother Lot, and his goods, and the women also, and the people.
GENESIS 14:16

There is an amusing, but completely legendary story about President Benjamin Harrison seeing a destitute man, a victim of the depression, plucking and eating blades of grass from the White House lawn. According to the story, the only thing the president did was to suggest that the man go around back where the grass was longer.

Abraham exemplified true compassion in dealing with those in need. When he learned that Lot had been captured he gathered 318 men and rescued Lot and the other captives. He saw a need and did something about it. John tells us in his First Epistle that if we see our brother in need and will not help him, the love of God does not dwell in us. We must be keepers of our kin whether they be our physical relatives or brothers and sisters in Christ.

It was Abraham Lincoln who said, "When any church will inscribe over its altar, as its sole qualification for membership, the Savior's condensed statement of both Law and Gospel, 'Thou shalt love the Lord thy God with all thy heart … and thy neighbor as thyself,' that church I will join with all my soul."

*T*ruth: I am my brother's keeper.

Well of tears

Who passing through the valley of Baca
make it a well; the rain also filleth the pools.
They go from strength to strength ...
PSALM 84:6, 7

For centuries the "Valley of Baca" has been known as the "valley of weeping." The name was derived from balsam trees in this valley that exude drops of resin, suggesting tears. Therefore, in the colorful language of the East when one goes through a deep crisis of life, he is going through the "Valley of Baca."

God promises not only that He will be with us in the "valley of weeping" but He will also actually turn the frustrations of this valley into a well of living water. He promises that those traveling this lonely vale will come out "going from strength to strength." There is a strange alchemy in tears, which makes us deeper in spirit, richer in compassion, more tender in daily expressions to one another. The one who travels this valley indeed finds his tears turn into a well of joy.

Many going through heartbreaks testify to tranquility transcending burden. Like David, they say, "He restoreth my soul." Myriads have emerged from "Baca" and have given to us beautiful music, majestic poetry, deep moving hymns learned there. Succeeding generations have been blessed by their trials.

*T*ruth: "They that sow in tears shall reap in joy" (Ps. 126:5).

Empty hands

---·⌒~·---

"So is he that layeth up treasure for himself, and is not rich toward God."
LUKE 12:21

On his deathbed Alexander the Great reportedly commanded that when he died, his hands should not be wrapped as was the custom of the day, but should be left exposed so that all men might see they were empty. He wanted everyone to realize that although he had ruled the world and had gained much of the world's riches, yet he left life as a common beggar, taking nothing with him. He went to meet his God with empty hands.

Strange, isn't it that men should hoard and sell their souls for that which they must lose.

Jesus helped two brothers face up to their greed by telling a story of the futility of wealth. The climax of that tale of the foolish braggart building new bars is arresting: "God said unto him, Thou fool, this night thy soul shall be required of thee: then whose shall those things be, which thou has provided?"

God does not condemn wealth. But He does condemn the misappropriation of wealth and man's misplaced values. Christ desires that we do not spend our time and energy seeking to be rich in this world's goods. He tells us to be "rich toward God." Put your emphasis on things eternal.

*T*ruth: He is no fool who gives up what he cannot keep to gain what he cannot lose.

Lined up to die

⟨⟨⟩⟩

Today's Scripture: 1 Corinthians 15

O death, where is thy sting?
O grave, where is thy victory?
1 CORINTHIANS 15:55

"Twenty-nine persons lined up to die this morning at New York's Kennedy Airport." With these words one reporter began his account of a recent fatal airline crash.

Everyone in the world is more or less "lined up to die." As one man said, "It's not a question of *if* we are going to die, but *when* we are going to die." This realization causes a cold wind of fear to blow about our head.

However, those who have found Christ have learned of another line in which they stand – the line of the living. Because Christ died and conquered death we have been made heirs of eternal life.

Death is not a terminal point. It is a doorway through which believers step into a richer and fuller life. The central fact of the New Testament is that Christ was raised from the dead and in His resurrection we can look forward to life. Paul emphatically asserts that death has lost its sting and its victory. No wonder believers have deep happiness and security in their faith.

Truth: All of life has meaning because Christ came and conquered death.

Clouds without rain

———— ⌒⌒⌒ ————

Today's Scripture: Jude

Clouds they are without water,
carried about of the winds (v. 12).

One of the weirdest phenomenon of celebrated Death Valley is its rainstorms that never reach the ground. Author Ben Lucien Burman told of one, "I saw an ominous black cloud in the distant sky. Long streamers of rain streaked down against the horizon." He hurried not wanting to get caught in a flash flood but to his amazement no water fell. The air was so dry and hot that the rain evaporated before hitting the ground. No doubt many weary travelers have looked with thankfulness to promising clouds only to have their hopes dashed by these dry rainstorms.

In explaining the evil of false teachers, Jude says they are clouds without water. One can imagine experiencing a long drought and, when eagerly anticipated clouds finally come, they pass over without spilling that precious liquid on the thirsty earth. Those who promise salvation by any other means than Jesus Christ are just as these clouds – promising much, delivering nothing.

We are in an age of spiritual drought. The war-weary and heart-hungry are thirsting for spiritual relief. By following our own high-sounding yet futile philosophies, we can let them die in their frustration. Or, as believers, we can give them a drink of living water that quenches all thirst. But, that living water cannot be diluted by the false philosophies of man.

*P*rayer: Lord, help us not to be clouds without water. Rather, let us be those who draw from the wells of salvation.

Freedom is fragile

⎯⎯⎯⎯ ⨲ ⎯⎯⎯⎯

Today's Scripture: Galatians 5:13-26

Stand fast therefore in the liberty wherewith
Christ hath made us free, and be not
entangled again with the yoke of bondage.
GALATIANS 5:1

Ten years of terror followed the freeing of the Congo from Belgium domination. Authorities estimated at least five hundred thousand people lost their lives in that war-torn country which was given the opportunity of self-government. Today, calm has been restored with the capable, but dictatorial rule of Joseph Mobutu. The Congolese learned freedom is a fragile flower easily crushed.

Paul too knew the traps of freedom as well as its joys. He was first to assure new Christians there was no longer bondage to some of the ceremonies that had been placed on them by self-serving religious leaders. Yet, at the same time, he sounded a warning that our freedom in Christ not be used as an excuse for sin. Such freedom would bind us again to habits and horrors of the past.

While the Bible gives broad principles, rather than minute rules, still it would be well for us to analyze our actions carefully so that we do not give occasion to sin. Peter suggested not using our freedom for a "cloak of maliciousness" (1 Pet. 2:16). Paul notes that in our actions we are not to offend others (1 Cor. 8:9). With these guidelines we can make intelligent decisions for our Christian actions in a world which is increasingly difficult to live in.

*P*rayer: Father, keep me true to You and pure in heart.

Approving words

"Well done, thou good and faithful servant: thou hast been faithful over a few things, I will make thee ruler over many things."

MATTHEW 25:21

An actor once told of a horrible nightmare he had in which he was telling funny stories and singing songs to a crowded audience – but no one clapped or laughed. He said, "It was terrible. Even at $100,000 a week such a situation would be hell on earth."

One of the built-in needs of man is that of approval and appreciation. In the parable of those charged with responsibility we learn much about God's appreciation for those who work faithfully in His vineyard. Note that He gives careful appreciation for the task we've done. The songwriter captured this moment in this beautiful verse, "All the talents I have, I have laid at Thy feet. Thy approval shall be my reward."

As in most relationships between God and man, we can use this principle in dealing with others. Words of kindness and appreciation can do much to make life easier and most palatable for others. Fulton Oursler suggested there is magic in a word of praise. I have a friend who writes cards to casual acquaintances just expressing appreciation for their friendship and to note he is praying for them. Many have been blessed by the small but unselfish act.

*P*rayer: Father, help me to look beyond my own selfishness to give appreciation and approval to others.

Stolen waters

―――― ⟨⟨⟨⟨ ――――

Today's Scripture: Proverbs 9:1-12

Stolen waters are sweet,
and bread eaten in secret is
pleasant. But he knoweth
not that the dead are there.
PROVERBS 9:17, 18

When young Caridad Mercader decided to escape her dull life as housewife and mother, she moved to Paris and joined the Communist party working in the underground. Later, she sent for her young son and trained him in intrigue. He grew up to be the celebrated assassin of Leon Trotsky, co-framer of communism, who had fallen out of favor with Stalin. Too late Mrs. Mercader saw her exciting world crumble and she was left in disillusionment. Her son in prison, her dreams crushed, her health gone, now stooped and old, she confided to a friend. "We have been deceived. This is not paradise. It is hell."

Millions have echoed Mrs. Mercader's frustration. "There is a way which seemeth right unto a man, but the end thereof are the ways of death" (Prov. 14:12). Too late many learn the lure of the bright lights and the sound of exciting music is cotton candy melting in disappointment when taken. In it is no substance but only that which is harmful.

The wise Proverbist noted, "Bread of deceit is sweet to a man; but afterwards his mouth shall be filled with gravel" (20:17). It is the wise man who refuses to be swept up with the enchantments of sin and sets his goals on pleasing Christ.

Truth: "Whatsoever a man soweth, that shall he also reap" (Gal. 6:7).

The life-wish

Today's Scripture: 1 Corinthians 15:35-44

So also is the resurrection of the dead.
It is sown in corruption;
it is raised in incorruption.
1 CORINTHIANS 15:42

Nearly two centuries before Christ a Greek mathematician named the seven wonders of the world. Philon of Byzantium said they were: the Great Pyramid of Khufu; the Lighthouse at Alexandria, the Hanging Gardens of Babylon, the Temple of Diana at Ephesus, Phidias, statue of Zeus at Olympia, the Mausoleum at Halicarnassus, and the Colossus of Rhodes. Today only the Great Pyramid stands intact as a monument to man's skill and to his longing for immortality. The Pyramid is a tomb.

Since life first appeared and Adam sinned, man has been preoccupied with death. Job wondered if man lived beyond the grave. The apostles' story of the resurrection was so dynamic because Christ forever proved immortality was no longer just a "life-wish" but a reality. For the last two thousand years we have been living with the peace that eternity awaits those who love Christ.

Paul deals with the problem of death in his letter to Corinth. He talks of the necessity of death and then how the body will be raised. He speaks of the mysteries of the God-given body and the state of living in a spiritual body. With resounding assurance, we too can add that because Christ lives, we live also. Our wish is more than hope, it is fact.

*T*ruth: We serve a risen Savior, He's in the world today.

Greater than gold

Today's Scripture: Psalm 19

More to be desired are they than gold:
yea, than much fine gold: sweeter also
than honey and the honeycomb.
PSALM 19:10

I visited a gold mine in South Africa and was intrigued by how much money, machinery, and men it takes to extract just ounces of gold from the earth. Although millions are spent in effort, only two thousand tons of gold are mined annually in all the world. If all the gold known to exist above ground – some $65 billion worth – were melted into a single block, its size would be about only that of a large barn.

Throughout history men have murdered

and plundered for gold. Wars have been waged for it and people's lives given in sacrifice for its possession. Today all countries use it in their trade and to settle accounts. World banks store it as a reserve for paper currency. In many countries, like the U.S.A., it is unlawful to possess gold except as jewelry. Man has had a long fascination and love affair with gold. That is right standing with God through His laws and judgments.

Gold and all other material things will pass away but God's Word endures forever. If men would spend as much time in pursuit of God's spiritual laws and peace, paradise would indeed be ours. Indeed, "in the keeping of them there is great reward" (v. 11).

*T*ruth: Materialism ends in despair and death while living in Christ is life and peace.

My boy

Today's Scripture: Romans 5:6-21

*But God commandeth his love
toward us, in that, while we were
yet sinners, Christ died for us.*
ROMANS 5:8

While dedicating a recreational home for
boys, philanthropist Horace Mann remarked,
"If all the money and all the energy you have
expended results in the salvation of only one
boy, it will not have been in vain." Afterward
one of the contributors chided, "My dear Mr.
Mann, weren't you exaggerating a bit when
you said all would be worthwhile if we saved
just one boy?" To this Mann replied instantly,
"Not if he were my boy."

In my imagination I can see Satan chiding

God, "Don't You think You're wasting time and effort with mankind? Why send Your Son to die for their sins? Many won't accept Him anyway." It seems as though God replies in love that if only one would accept redemption it would be worthwhile because of His intense personal love for individuals. In our world of mass production and the population explosion, the individual seems to be shrinking in importance. However, from the first page of God's Book to the last we are assured how much He loves each of us. One cannot help but feel that if he were the only human on earth, God still would have sent His Son Jesus to redeem him.

It is easy to make decisions of destiny for people we do not know or love. But, when we get emotionally involved in their lives, we begin to care for them. Thank God He cared for us.

*P*rayer: Help me, God, to care for others as You care for me.

The still

Today's Scripture: Psalm 46

Be still, and know that I am God … The Lord of hosts is with us; the God of Jacob is our refuge.
PSALM 46:10, 11

When disaster strikes a British navy vessel, the "still" is instantly sounded. It is a warning device that simply means: "Prepare to do the wise thing." When an emergency comes, few know what to do, but in moments of calm enforced by the signal, each man finds his responsibility and functions accordingly. By sounding the "still" confusion is averted and many tragedies prevented.

When tragedies or emergencies arise in our lives, we seldom know how to cope with them. For these occasions God has the "still" which should be sounded, "Be still and know that I am God." In the calmness of His presence we can learn direction, receive strength, and meet the situation.

Most of us are worrywarts. Like the disciples we worry about the future and if we will be able to stand under all sorts of living pressures. Again, He sounds the "still": "Stand in awe, and sin not: commune with your own heart upon your bed, and be still" (Ps. 4:4). Observing the "still" is not a neurotic escape from reality. Rather, it is receiving instructions and inspiration from Him who has all of us in His hands.

*T*ruth: Like sparrows crossing a freeway by hopping, we do not realize we have the power to rise above the dangers by being borne up in His protecting arms.

What does God do?

Today's Scripture: Isaiah 61:1-3

Then said Jesus to them again,
"Peace be unto you:
as my Father hath sent me,
even so send I you."
JOHN 20:21

A little boy asked his father, "What does God do all day?" Unknown to the lad, this is a deep theological question. To some, God made the world as an inventor would a machine, then stood back and is watching it work. To others, God is deeply involved in His creation and influences it by His Spirit. The Bible assures us the latter view is the correct one.

Even a casual reading of Scripture indicates how deeply involved God is with His creation. He so loved the world He gave His only Son that the world through Him might be brought back into fellowship with the Father. That involvement did not stop with the Ascension of Christ into Heaven. God sent His Holy Spirit to continue the work of influence and fellowship.

Nowhere is Christ's mission so clearly defined as in Isaiah 61. He came to preach good tidings, to bind up the broken-hearted, to proclaim liberty to captives, to comfort those who mourn. His mission is also our mission. God is still involved in His creation through His Holy Spirit and through us, His chosen children. By our influence and love, we can show the world what God does all day.

*T*ruth: God continually influences us to heal the hurts of mankind and to point them Godward.